anythink

D1165625

WHEN YOU WANT TO CROSS THE STREET, LOOK BOTH WAYS

Retold by NICHOLAS IAN

Illustrated by DIEGO FUNCK

Music Arranged and Produced by MUSICAL YOUTH PRODUCTIONS

CANTATA
LEARNING

WWW.CANTATALEARNING.COM

CANTATA
LEARNING

Published by Cantata Learning
1710 Roe Crest Drive
North Mankato, MN 56003
www.cantatalearning.com

Copyright © 2017 Cantata Learning

A note to educators and librarians from the publisher: Cantata Learning has provided the following data to assist in book processing and suggested use of Cantata Learning product.

Publisher's Cataloging-in-Publication Data
Prepared by Librarian Consultant: Ann-Marie Begnaud
Library of Congress Control Number: 2015958191
    When You Want to Cross the Street, Look Both Ways
    Series: Tangled Tunes : On the Move
    Retold by Nicholas Ian
    Illustrated by Diego Funck
    Summary: Sing about safety in this twist on a classic song.
    ISBN: 978-1-63290-602-1 (library binding/CD)
    ISBN: 978-1-63290-655-7 (paperback/CD)
Suggested Dewey and Subject Headings:
    Dewey: E 363.12
    LCSH Subject Headings: Transportation – Safety measures – Juvenile literature. | Pedestrian crosswalks – Juvenile literature. | Traffic safety – Juvenile literature. | Cycling – Safety measures – Juvenile literature. | Transportation – Songs and music – Texts. | Pedestrian crosswalks – Songs and music – Texts. | Traffic safety – Songs and music – Texts. | Cycling – Safety measures – Songs and music – Texts. | Transportation – Safety measures – Juvenile sound recordings. | Pedestrian crosswalks – Juvenile sound recordings. | Traffic safety – Juvenile sound recordings. | Cycling – Safety measures – Juvenile sound recordings.
    Sears Subject Headings: Transportation. | Safety education. | School songbooks. | Children's songs. | World music.
    BISAC Subject Headings: JUVENILE NONFICTION / Health & Daily Living / Safety. | JUVENILE NONFICTION / Music / Songbooks. | JUVENILE NONFICTION / Transportation / General.

Book design and art direction, Tim Palin Creative
Editorial direction, Flat Sole Studio
Music direction, Elizabeth Draper
Music arranged and produced by Musical Youth Productions

Printed in the United States of America in North Mankato, Minnesota.
072016   0335CGF16

ACCESS THE MUSIC!

SCAN CODE WITH MOBILE APP

CANTATALEARNING.COM

Staying safe when you are out and about is important. Before you cross a street, look both ways. You need to **buckle up** when riding in a car. While **pedaling** your bike, wear a **helmet**.

To learn more about staying safe, turn the page and sing along!

When you want to cross the street, look both ways.
Left, right, left!

When you want to cross the street, look both ways.
Left, right, left!

Before you cross the street, stop, listen, and take a peek. When you want to cross the street, look both ways.

When you want to cross the street, look both ways. Left, right, left!

When you want to cross the street, look both ways. Left, right, left!

Before you cross the street, stop, listen, and take a peek.
When you want to cross the street, look both ways.

When you get in the car, buckle up.
Click, click!

When you get in the car, buckle up.
Click, click!

Before you drive away, make sure you stay safe. When you get in the car, buckle up.

When you get in the car, buckle up.
    Click, click!

When you get in the car, buckle up.
    Click, click!

12

Before you drive away, make sure you stay safe.

When you get in the car, buckle up.

When you're riding on your bike, wear a helmet.
Ding, ding!

When you're riding on your bike, wear a helmet.
Ding, ding!

Protect your head, and you'll be glad you did.
When you're riding on your bike, wear a helmet.

When you're riding on your bike, wear a helmet.
Ding, ding!

When you're riding on your bike, wear a helmet.
Ding, ding!

Protect your head, and you'll be glad you did.
When you're riding on your bike, wear a helmet.

Before you ride across the street, stop and look.
Left, right, left!

Before you ride across the street, stop and look.
Left, right, left!

18

Even when the light is green,

    make sure you check the **scene**.

Before you ride across the street, stop and look.

Before you ride across the street, stop and look.
Left, right, left!

Before you ride across the street, stop and look.
Left, right, left!

Even when the light is green,
   make sure you check the scene.
Before you ride across the street, stop and look.

SONG LYRICS
When You Want to Cross the Street, Look Both Ways

When you want to cross the street,
   look both ways.
Left, right, left!
When you want to cross the street,
   look both ways.
Left, right, left!

Before you cross the street, stop, listen,
   and take a peek.
When you want to cross the street,
   look both ways.

When you want to cross the street,
   look both ways.
Left, right, left!
When you want to cross the street,
   look both ways.
Left, right, left!

Before you cross the street, stop, listen,
   and take a peek.
When you want to cross the street,
   look both ways.

When you get in the car, buckle up.
Click, click!

When you get in the car, buckle up.
Click, click!

Before you drive away, make sure
   you stay safe.
When you get in the car, buckle up.

When you get in the car, buckle up.
Click, click!

When you get in the car, buckle up.
Click, click!

Before you drive away, make sure
   you stay safe.
When you get in the car, buckle up.

When you're riding on your bike,
   wear a helmet.
Ding, ding!

When you're riding on your bike,
   wear a helmet.
Ding, ding!

Protect your head, and you'll be glad
   you did.
When you're riding on your bike,
   wear a helmet.

When you're riding on your bike,
   wear a helmet.
Ding, ding!

When you're riding on your bike,
   wear a helmet.
Ding, ding!

Protect your head, and you'll be glad
   you did.
When you're riding on your bike,
   wear a helmet.

Before you ride across the street, stop
   and look.
Left, right, left!

Before you ride across the street, stop
   and look.
Left, right, left!

Even when the light is green, make
   sure you check the scene.
Before you ride across the street, stop
   and look.

Before you ride across the street, stop
   and look.
Left, right, left!

Before you ride across the street, stop
   and look.
Left, right, left!

Even when the light is green, make
   sure you check the scene.
Before you ride across the street, stop
   and look.

When You Want to Cross the Street, Look Both Ways

Indie Pop (World/Folk)
Musical Youth Productions

Verse 4 (2x)
Before you ride across the street, stop and look.
Left, right, left!
Before you ride across the street, stop and look.
Left, right, left!
Even when the light is green, make sure you check the scene.
Before you ride across the street, stop and look.

GLOSSARY

buckle up—fasten your seatbelt

helmet—a hard, protective covering for your head

pedaling—moving a bicycle by working the pedals with your feet

protect—to keep safe

scene—a place where something happens

GUIDED READING ACTIVITIES

1. This song is about staying safe when you are getting around your city or town. What safety rules did you sing about?

2. Think of some other places where it might be important to stay safe. What do you do to stay safe at home or at school?

3. What is your favorite way to get around your neighborhood? Draw a picture of yourself walking, biking, or getting around in some other way.

TO LEARN MORE

Anderson, Steven. *Wheels on the Bus*. Mankato, MN: Cantata Learning, 2016.

Ipcizade, Catherine. *H Is for Honk! A Transportation Alphabet*. Mankato, MN: Capstone Press, 2011.

Lyons, Shelly. *Signs in My Neighborhood*. Mankato, MN: Capstone Press, 2013.

Lyons, Shelly. *Transportation in My Neighborhood*. Mankato, MN: Capstone Press, 2013.